Toward Repentance

Fr. Seraphim El Baramosy

Toward Repentance

Fr. Seraphim El Baramosy

Toward Repentance

Seraphim El Baramosy
Seraphim.elbaramosy@asfcs.org

Translated by Theresa Shehata
Edited by Lisa Agaiby

1st edition in Arabic (2010) 1st edition in English (2017)

A S F C S

Alexandria School Foundation for Christian Studies www.bookstore.asfcs.org
ISBN 978-1-950831-07-4

HIS HOLINESS POPE TAWADROS II
118th Pope and Patriarch of the See of Alexandria

HIS GRACE BISHOP ISIDORE
Bishop and Abbot of the Monastery of Saint Mary – Baramos

Contents

My beloved, please, in the name of Jesus Christ seek your salvation.

Saint Antony

●●●

Repentance is shown not only passionately but also quickly.

Saint Ambrose

Introduction

●●●

Life today has become a valley of anxiety, and today's person is more restless than ever before. Civilization and the metamorphosis of life into a consumer society, have changed the characteristics of human behavior; they have directly affected thinking, decisions, contentment and priorities. Hence, one is torn between what they see and what they want. Even the human will itself has been affected by civilization and consumer culture, becoming weak, unsettled, absent and dependent. Eventually, this has led to alienation that has become entrenched in the heart of human beings. Although the aims of the Renaissance were happiness, comfort and human welfare, they became a thorn in one's being that could not be removed, for the cosmic roles were re-assigned to make the human the center of existence. Accordingly, he had to overstep the powers within his life to achieve stability in the universe, in nature, and within himself, and this is something beyond one's capabilities. Hence, an affective anxiety formed and crept into the human's being, that grew to become a restless, unstoppable, entity-related anxiety that surrounds one at all times. Such anxiety separates a person from his personality and blurs his insight into his role in life and meaning of existence. Anxiety, according to the Danish philosopher Søren Kierkegaard, is "the precise definition of sin." It is a ramification of sin taking root in the human entity and what follows, including a person's alienation from God. Sin is a human tension that arises when we deviate from our path and distort our image through associating with the world, seeking satisfaction within our earthly lifespan, and temporarily enjoying the pleasures of the senses. This tension continues as long as a person is convinced that he is the center of his life and refuses to give the helm to God once again. Accordingly, Saint Macarius the Great said, "falling in the dreadful adversity of sin."

Our current calamity is that we have moved away from being God's image by attempting to create our personal identity and draw our individual portrait apart from God. Yet, what does not cross our minds is that there is no absolute centralism for one in life. It is the centralism of Satan who hides behind one's aspirations and ambitions. When we do not make God the center of our lives, then we give the helm to Satan who deceives us into believing that we alone possess the right to choose and make decisions in life without divine intervention.

Here we realize that the only solution to dispel anxiety from our human entity is to let God take control and once again crown our whole life. This is the inclusive definition of repentance, which will be our focus in the coming pages.

Pursuing Hope

●●●

It is a perplexing question that echoes in agonizing hearts yearning to live the life of righteousness, why transgressions become entangled within the delicate human entity. A question that the self poses in astonishment, when the will eagerly desires to follow in the steps of the Lord. But the self falls and is defeated during its daily experience and finds the spirit of sadness swirling around a heart that has lost its heaven and its purity during the conflict between righteousness and sinfulness.

The insistence of this question intensifies when you find yourself moving one step on the path of light and your insight deepens during moments of earnest prayer about eternity. In ecstasy, you begin to witness the delight and glory of a life hidden in Jesus Christ, but suddenly you hit a stumbling block that stops your journey: a block that was thrown on the path by a sinful hand. You begin to see a trap hidden under your good intentions and honorable objectives, into which you fall and are transported to a dark, narrow cellar where a demonic spirit is hovering over the cold, wet doorstep. It is the cellar of sin that leads to death!

When you have an insatiable hunger for new life, you find that the people around you urge you to read the word of God in order to perceive the captivating beauty coming out of the lines, letters and words. While seeds of life start to form the initial shoots of the new human being, according to the logic of the intangible Kingdom of God inside your heart, you will find thorns coming forth to catch these shoots and destroy them while they are still young and have not started their way toward the light, so long as the soul is inattentive to God's commandment.

Hence, you hasten to enter your chamber of prayer in order to shed tears, and find the Savior's arms always open, and where you will feel delight and comfort filling your heart, as if you have left this world and climbed up Mount Tabor; the place where the gleam of glory overwhelms those in attendance and reveals the secrets of the Kingdom to the eyes of the soul.

Once you go out of the chamber of prayer, you will please the Savior by saying the words of Peter who said on the Mount of Transfiguration, "Lord, it is good for us to be here" (Matt 17:4). Here you will find joy, support, glory and strength, and hope will become a reality through the Lord's presence. However, the world, time and the flesh refuse to let the soul be distant from the world. And so reluctantly, the soul descends the mount of glory represented in prayers, to confront a life that is mingled with absurd threads of lust, power, pleasure and money blended within a world of wickedness. Together they form a giant that treads with diabolical harshness on every soul immersed in invisible hope, and every soul that adheres in life to the path and law of love.

Go to church, where the gathering of God's people are united together, and your prayers will combine with the prayers of the body of Christ, and the Spirit that is present in the church will present them to the Father who will bless the congregation and grant them a token of the new life: the body and blood of Jesus. Accordingly, the soul will become stronger and feel as if it possesses the Kingdom! Sin will have no place, and Satan will declare his defeat before the glory of salvation that has settled in the hearts of those who possess the sacrament of life that is presented by the Eucharist.

However, it will not be long before you notice the lusts of the flesh arising again, the temptations of life creeping up once more, and the world's demands yet again weave a cloak of dust that stands in the way of your soul advancing on its path toward God. Thus, the soul is prevented from moving toward the Lord, by whom we are beloved, though we be lofty and self-adoring.

Life Paradox

●●●

Amid all the conflicts surrounding the soul, it wonders: is there a solution for sin? Will Satan and his cronies face complete defeat? Will there be an eternal light that shines as a sign that life rejects darkness?

While confused, and in anticipation of answers to your questions, you will hear a quiet, soft voice echoing in the depths of your heart saying: "While the earth remains, seedtime and harvest, cold and heat, winter and summer, and day and night shall not cease." Suddenly, you will realize that these words are the Lord's in the Book of Genesis (8:22). The Lord said these words when the Flood ended, after He--instead of destroying humankind--bore their indulgence in wickedness that had penetrated the human entity since the day of the fall. And so now, one leads a life between light and darkness. Life has become to all humankind, full of paradoxes—paradoxes between:

Falling and rising up,

Estrangement and unity,

Defeat and victory,

Sorrow and joy,

15

Hardship and ease,

Groaning and delight,

Death and life,

Flesh and spirit,

Ego and the other,

Individualism and personalism,

Being and possession,

Finite and infinite,

Nothingness and existence,

Time and eternity.

It is a relative life that we live: a mixture of contradictions. Dust adjoins soul in the human being— this is the real life that the Holy Spirit wants us to perceive and learn. Life is not one-sided; it is neither only intensely materialistic, or only spiritual. Rather, it is a set of paradoxes. Amid the paradoxes that we face on our existential journey, our tendency toward one side of life, and our struggle to be freed from the other side, constitutes our human orientation.

Thus we should pay attention to that which, after the fall, spoiled the whole nature: sin which crept into the heart of human beings. Therefore, the illusion of impeccable crystal purity, is an unattainable dream as long as we are prisoners of time and the world. In addition, God does not demand results back from us, but He calls us to act and defend our salvation.

The purity we should strive for is the result of a hitherto constant struggle. This conflict is the one that draws the Spirit's free gifts to us, sealing them with purity and chastity. However, the penetration of the heart by the Spirit is conditional upon our vigilance, cries, and hope in seeking aid and salvation. Furthermore, our call, which perpetuates day and night and comes out of the depths of our hearts that wait for a beam of light, and is amid harsh clouds of sins, becomes: "Please come, dwell in us, and purify us from all unrighteousness" (Tierce, the Hourly Prayers). It is the Spirit that purifies us from unrighteousness and sin, not our struggle. So, avoiding the dismissal of the Spirit from our lives, should be the goal of every struggle against the enemies of light. Hence, the Infinite's demand from us is not that we are rid of sins, but rather, that we struggle against it. The removal of sins, however, is the fruit that the Spirit reaps in us from the tree of life, by which every person who eats thereof will live forever.

Here we can know that the secret of washing away sins lies in our vigilance during the continued conflict and perseverance to be rid of all sins that are attached to our pure vestment that we wore on the day of our baptism. Accordingly, there is no purity without conflict with darkness, because we are threatened constantly by enemies that do not sleep, rest or become fed up with frequent defeat.

The Paradox of Repentance

•••

Repentance itself is one of life's paradoxes, consisting of tendency and struggle in unison. It is a tendency to consult with the Spirit to return to God, and it is, at the same time, a struggle against Satan's chains that stand in the way of such a move toward God. It represents an inner contradiction in the human heart: we desire to draw closer to the divine light, but this leads to a painful revelation of the sin-stained soul which is a result of submission to the world and its materialistic law. This light slowly uncovers the darkness, leaving us in a state of continued struggle between hope and the dread of approaching God; between longing for Him and the fear of meeting Him!

Regarding this struggle, that the soul passes through when the light of God shines in the horizons of the Spirit, the Russian archimandrite Sophrony Sakharov explains in his book titled *We Shall See Him As He Is*:

[...] The man becomes torn;

From one side, he is steeped in fright

Concerning seeing himself

Filled with repugnance

From the other side,

He feels tremendous power

That he did not recognize before,

Resulting from seeing the living Lord...

In his book *The Inner Kingdom*, Kallistos Ware wrote:

Repentance that is filled with grief,

Yet at the same time filled with joy,

Expresses the creative tension

Found at all times

In the Christian life on this earth.

Indeed, this essential paradox constituting our repentance, is the creative tension that painfully discerns the truth of the self and the divine light that shines within it. It yearns to meet with God, forgetting itself, its state and its own reality. These are preliminary steps that the self takes to move toward the Lord that guard against traps of despair that are set up for the sinner when he announces his return to the bosom of the Father again.

The feelings of repentance always waver between two pivots:

- The pivot of light (present): represents the self's delight with returning to the Lord.
- The pivot of darkness (of the past): represents the self's agony over the wounds it caused to the heart of God when it committed sins.

Although the pivot of light reflects the soul during its desired meeting with God – as it forgets its truth while being in the midst of the warmth and compassion of God--the pivot of the soul's bygone darkness is its guarantee not to be haughty when feelings of spiritual excellence become its obsession. The present divine light shields the self from despair, while the darkness of the self protects it from spiritual superiority and mental haughtiness.

It is the same notion of love/fear (awe) with which we meet God. If fear drains away, our will is weakened with regard to abiding by the Bible as well as resisting sins; and if love dwindles, our Christianity is converted into new Paganism but with a more sophisticated behavioral dynamic. This is because the essence of God is love. If love ceased to be, we would convert to worshipping another god that is far from being the trinity of love.

The paradox of repentance, as Saint Augustine believes, simply is to love God and detest the self at the same time. Therefore, in Book II of his *Confessions*, when he prays, he says:

Oh ! How better is to confess in Your hands,

As when I admit my sins to You,

You send Your compassion,

Your beam of light to me

I feel ashamed of myself then,

And I see myself worthy of hatred,

But You deserve love,

In You I should put my thoughts,

Emotions and desires.

Hence, the paradox of repentance, is necessary because it consists of and is filled with joy and pain, as described by Kallistos Ware.

Does this mean that we have to accept the existence of sin in our life? Far from it! We, nonetheless must realize the struggle we face, the nature of the enemies waiting for us, the nature of the conflict itself, as well as our own human natures, so that we can rise up after having fallen, and resist and achieve victory after being defeated. We must understand that sin besieges our nature as a whole, creeps into the heart to find a place where it can settle and evolve. It waits for moments of apathy, boredom, laziness, confusion or weakness to creep into and shackle the soul with chains of hell and death. According to the Scriptures, a person is inclined toward evil from an early age. Consequently, no one escapes sin throughout the ages. What God demands from us is the action, not the outcome; struggle, not salvation.

Saint Paul the Apostle also spoke about an inner dual conflict between the will and deed; between the heart's longing and the inertia of life. We find this in his epistle to the Romans, in which he bemoaned on behalf of all the mankind, saying: "For even though the desire to do good is in me, I am not able to do it" (Rom 7:8).

This conflict, which is inside one's will, is already the focus of human struggle. It hopes for eternal light and the clothing of virtue on the one hand, and the action stained by trespasses and sins on the other. Victory lies in the struggle and it is by grace that we are crowned, through this struggle, with purity and liberation from sin. Therefore, doing away with the bottomless pit is a result of partnership between one's continuous struggle and the grace that supports and rewards.

So do not let weakness and fall discourage you. Do not cease crying out to God so that you may obtain the grace of liberation, and as long as your heart calls out, you are a victor. You are defeated only when you stop crying out and struggling, in hope of victory.

We find this concept clearly in the prayers recited by the priest before the liturgical service of the Eucharist (Liturgy of Saint Basil , The Preparation Prayer):

> O Lord, who knows the hearts of every one,
> Who is Holy and who rests
> In the midst of His saints,
> Who alone is without sin,
> And who is mighty to forgive sins,
> You know, O Lord, I am unworthy,
> And unprepared,
> And undeserving of this sacred service
> That is Yours,
> And I have no boldness that I should draw near
> And open my mouth before Your holy glory,
> But according to the multitude of Your tender
> mercies,
> Forgive me, a sinner ...

The prayer before the Most Holy One, which is filled with deep contrition, is already on the tongue of all the penitents who have not reached their full liberation from sin. Their permanent and continuous cry is, "In Your deep compassion forgive me, I am a sinner." That cry alone is the secret of victory for the sinner over the self that wants to be righteous, and over Satan who wants to deceive the self with its righteousness, and at other times with its futility of standing before God. It is prayer that makes a person ready to stand before God, since it dresses one in a gown woven with delicate and pleasant humility.

On the other side, we find that the paradoxes present within us every day, hour and moment, are the main reasons for our growth and maturity. Without black, white would not be the symbol of purity and chastity; without darkness, nature would not rejoice at the light; without fight and conflict, human beings would not celebrate victory. Crowning comes only after fighting. The real taste of victory lies in the appreciation of the effort exerted during the conflict. These are the teachings that Saint Moses the Black was keen to pass on to everyone who came to him complaining about the ferocity of warfare. He would say:

Without wars and fighting,

Virtue would not be.

Virtue is the fruit of the burning conflict between matter and spirit, when the human's spirit tends to rise above the constant and permanent attraction of matter. The final crown will not be placed upon heads that were not wet with sweat in the quest of daily struggle. Furthermore, victory will only be reserved for those who were able to say "no" to the present world that is subjected by evil.

In fact, the conflict between the flesh and the spirit rages in the micro-cosmos inside the human entity. It occurs between devilish thoughts—that sneak in during moments of inattentiveness to the conscience, and draws the human toward the bottomless pit, taking the form of sin—and the whispers of the Holy Spirit that wants to inflame the heart whose wick is about to go out, so that he could see the light of life again.

This war is in the mind and heart of the human being and places him in a permanent state of disagreement between an enormous power that is visible by the insight of a pure spirit, and attracts all people to Him, and another power that uses bodily senses to win him over.

The human conflict does not stop, but the person, over time, gains greater insight into the truth and a growing realization of the pretense behind the fleshly instincts that is cloaked in a gown of pleasure; and this is a result of his growing faith and awareness through successive daily experience. As long as a person walks towards the light, the whispers of darkness that attract him become weakened; and as long as he, in turn, consents to the presence of Satanic deception in his eyes, the nets of darkness around his neck will increase, and he will become a prisoner in a state lacking meaning, value and purpose, and will be closer to the bottomless pit than to the Kingdom.

The Brazilian novelist Paulo Coelho in his book *Warrior of the Light* writes about the two powers that attract the soul:

> A warrior knows that an angel and a devil Are
> both competing for his sword hand.
> The devil says: "You will weaken.
> You will not know exactly when.
> You are afraid."
> The angel says: "You will weaken.
> You will not know exactly when.
> You are afraid."

The warrior is surprised.

Both angel and devil have said the same thing.

Then the devil goes on: "Let me help you." And the angel says: "I will help you."

At that moment,

The warrior understands the difference.

The words may be the same, but these two allies are completely different.

And he chooses the angel's hand.

Our victory, above all, is conditional upon our knowledge of the conflict, its parties, methods of victory and reasons for the defeat. Satan has used words of the Spirit in an attempt to deceive Christ, but Christ's awareness of the Spirit's intent of those words became the secret for defeating Satan during those wars that the mountain witnessed. Awareness means training the senses and sharpening the spiritual fighting skills through prayer, the word of God and the Eucharist. Most importantly, be humble as we are in the flesh.

Awareness

●●●

Our knowledge of these paradoxes surrounding us, increases our awareness of the reality in which we live, and makes us more aware of the likelihood that we might stumble and fall. By being content with our human nature, which is apt to making mistakes, we will become stronger and more able to rise again. What makes it hard for a person to rise again after falling, is a false feeling of firmness and stability as well as trust in a matured human nature. This nature may become agitated at any time, causing a tremendous shock when the person realizes his purity was stained by sins and that his stability was a dream that quickly passed by.

Therefore, Saint Paul the Apostle advises: "Therefore let him that thinks he stands take heed lest he fall" (1 Cor. 10:12).

Saint John Chrysostom says:

> When the arrogant falls, he feels surprised,
> Regrets and loses hope,
> Yet the humble person knows his weakness, Is
> not surprised by an action or behavior,

But regrets with fresh hope in the mercy of the Infinite.

Hence, it is necessary to marginalize errors and hindrances in the life we live, so that we can rise up quickly each time we fall, and so that each time we weaken in our daily violent struggle, we may act positively after every failure.

Our acceptance of ourselves is not reconciliation with sin but, rather, awareness of the fall, which we have as human beings that live in a tent; but this awareness should not be separated from the persistent quest to change that situation by the hand of grace. Frequently, some people struggle, having confidence in stability, without knowing the fragility of the human psyche. We are surrounded by serpents of sin at all times that lie waiting to strike us in the moment of our inattentiveness. We also find that there are people who are aware of their flawed nature, but they are not broken by the force of the fall, and hence, they do not work on changing their situation! Their awareness then leads to complacency and reconciliation with darkness.

In that case, it is essential for one to combine the awareness of human frailties with action, and to press on in the quest to rise, repent and be renewed. Thus, this repentance is supported by the power of hope that saves the sinner through his ongoing struggle and quest to rise again.

Every time a cloud of temptation comes to surround you and scatter your longing for purity, you must stand fast and hear the echo inside you:

It is the sinful human nature

That operates in me for death,

It is the wretched body

Which is trying to shackle my spirit

Rebelling at the physical world,

These are remnants of painful, falling moments

That grasped my parents Adam and Eve

In the far-off past,

But I will rise

In the grace of the new life,

That shined upon me in Christ Jesus,

Even though I walk through the darkest valley

I will not be afraid, or weakened,

Nor will I surrender

Arrows of enemies may wound me as they wish

But I will not leave the battle and hide,

My wounds will witness my struggle

On the day when the glory of Christ is revealed.

The New Creation

•••

We live life in a fragile vessel made of clay, which is our limited nature, but eagerness of heart is the secret to steadfastness against the harshness of life, and eagerness should become an action—an action that is carried out for the sake of God.

Christianity did not bring us a new external nature of a physical body in which to place our human entity in. A Christian's presence exists at the same time and spatial cycle in which the rest of creation lives. As human beings, we are all alike in what we have and what we do, according to the physical nature, for as Saint Peter the Apostle says, "the same afflictions are accomplished in your brethren that are in the world" (1 Peter 5:9). However, the new creation that Saint Paul the Apostle spoke about is just the image of God inscribed in the essence of our human being, looking like the face of Christ, only when our image is purified from the impurities of sin by the blood of the New Testament. Accordingly, it returns to its former pure and beautiful image as it had been before the fall, reflecting the bright, divine origin upon which it was likened.

A new creation in Christ is the key to opening humans' sight to comprehend resurrection beyond death. A small seed in a Christian's view is not an insignificant thing; rather it is a large, fruitful tree! This is the secret of new life. It is a renewal of the insight for life to see everything through the eyes of God dwelling within us. Consequently, we find that pain in a Christian's life, when marked by patience and hope in the Lord, is a crown of glory and a living testimony. In addition, we see that the fall is a push toward the resurrection by the greatest power; or, according to the immortal expression of Saint John Chrysostom, it is the secret "to return with greater vigor." And thus we find sin in the Christian dictionary, in spite of all its ugliness and negativity which reveals defeat in one's life, leads by repentance to a test in which we see the merciful face of God.

So, sin is the expression of humanity that is stained by the knowledge of good and evil by practical action and falling. On the other hand, it may result in a valuable chance through which we see the work of God, His unconditional love, and His salvation, which does not depend on our current attitude, but rather, they are heaped upon us according to the generosity of mercy in the heart of God toward us. However, we feel such mercy only when we begin to repent.

Sin without repentance is acceptance of judgment. Sin with repentance means seeing the unconditional grace in all God's actions toward us:

> And you, who once were alienated and enemies in your mind by wicked works, yet now He has reconciled in the body of His flesh through death, to present you holy, and blameless, and above reproach in His sight (Col 1: 21-22).

About this concept, Henri Boulad writes in his book *Inner Peace*:

> Grace needs a window through which
> The man's heart passes,
> The wound of sin is that window,
> That allows the grace to
> Deeply penetrate our hearts,
> To quench ourselves that are like the dry land...

The account of the tax collector is an example of that unique case of the work of grace: the wounds of sin filled the tax collector's soul with sadness; moans streamed in his heart as a river; the emptiness transmitted echoes of beatings on his chest that rocked heaven. Then simple words were spoken that opened the door to grace to justify and forgive.

> And the tax collector, standing afar off, would not so much as raise his eyes to heaven, but beat his breast, saying, 'God, be merciful to me a sinner!' (Luke 18: 13)

While reading the New Testament, we find that God has come in the flesh for the sake of sinners, not the righteous, for He said: "For I did not come to call the righteous, but sinners, to repentance" (Matt 9:13). Here, we can recognize that the righteous themselves are the furthest from seeing the merciful face of God, and tasting the unconditional grace. God's reproach to Scribes and Pharisees as well as leaders of the people is sufficient proof of the seriousness of self-righteousness that is always criticized by the Lord. Only the penitent can taste the mercy when he implores the Infinite to rescue him from the mire of sin. When a person realizes that he is nothing in confronting sin and confronting the powers of darkness, then he says together with Saint Antony the Great, when he stood against Satan and his cronies: "I am weaker than the youngest one of you". The weakness declared by Saint Antony is the weakness of the self and its human capabilities in the face of darkness; but this weakness turns into a tremendous, victorious vigor when grace intervenes and leads the self in this conflict, leaving the confrontation solely between God and Satan. Then all the forces of darkness weaken before the face of the Lord who shields those crying out to Him day and night.

Saint Athanasius wrote in his book *The Life of Antony* (chapters 10, 11) the details of the conflict between Antony and the demons, that ended when the Lord came directly to help him:

> In this way,
>
> He [Antony] looked up at the ceiling
>
> And saw the ceiling was opened,
>
> And rays of light were coming down.
>
> That moment, demons disappeared,
>
> And his bodily pain ceased,
>
> And the structure returned sound...

Saint Athanasius then adds:

> He came out on the next day having strong inclination to serve God.

Oh, I wish we could recognize the magnitude of the grace and help that surrounds us! Oh, I wish we could recognize the glory of victory that awaits our hearts' cries for God to enter our hearts! Only at that moment will sin not frighten us, nor bind us with the bars of despair, because our eyes will be fixed looking up to heaven, hoping for help and rejoicing in it. Standing before those who are looking toward the Invisible God, soldiers of evil can do nothing except flee to the bottomless pit—which is their destiny—in despair and defeat.

Repentance

●●●

One of the matters that we have to pay attention to, is that committing sins as a result of weakness is not like committing sins due to stubbornness or complacency. Obstinacy in committing sins makes the Spirit lose its ability to intervene to rescue that person. The example of Pharaoh, who resisted God's call for His people to go into the wilderness, is a testimony to human obstinacy that can lead the self to drowning and perdition.

On the other hand, the sinner kneels before the Lord uttering no words, for he does not know what to do. Previously he spoke and made promises and commitments, but sin broke all those promises and laid the soul bare in disgrace and shame in God's presence. Therefore, nothing remains for that person except to raise his eyes that are mixed with confusion, remorse and longing, toward heaven. His sight toward heaven become his silent prayer that speak of his state of confusion and hope: "We do not know what to do, but our eyes are upon You" (2 Chron 20:12). Because of this self that longs to do but cannot do, God strengthens it in its weakness, comforts its broken heart, and forgives it; for the Lord is tender with a contrite heart, downcast eyes, and the shedding of tears that hope for a new beginning.

It is repentance that opens the floodgates of heaven to pour forth spiritual rain (grace) for us, that quenches the desolate human spirit of its thirst for compassion.

Biblical repentance is not a state of sorrow, as much as it is a moment of realization of the reality of life, for the self sees truth and falsehood, and through this insight, comprehends light and darkness, and identifies the gap between the glory of heaven and pleasures of the world.

Repentance is a gaze toward heaven with fresh, renewed hope that is not hindered by the heaviness of sin nor stopped by the enormity of trespasses, because it's hope is in the trinity of love. Such a gaze toward the New Jerusalem attracts one to the intangible beauty that is the beauty of truth, light, and resurrection.

Repentance is not a negative attitude in which we cry over spilt milk without moving forward. Nor is it motionless moments during which we bemoan the past. Rather, it is a diligent movement that stimulates the self to change its stance on life and its three dimensions (the self, the other, and the Lord).

Although the body expresses them through tears and sighs, they are indeed moments of joy and peace.

However, the sighs and sadness of repentance are cheerful and filled with heartfelt peace. Thus, Saint Paul the Apostle articulated this delightful sorrow, saying, "For godly sorrow produces repentance leading to salvation, not to be regretted" (2 Cor 7:10). The penitence of salvation does not rest on remorse, yet it is based on positive, effective sorrow that is moving forward by the Spirit of God.

Søren Kierkegaard defines sin as anxiety. However, Merlot Borodin in her book titled *Mystery of the Gift of Tears in Eastern Christianity* writes, "Christian sorrow does not worry because it does not lose hope."

The difference between sorrow that arises from sin, and Christian sorrow which is based on God's will, is that the former is anxiety while the latter is sorrow without anxiety because it is filled with peace. This peace is due to having faith in God's goodness and forgiveness. Hence, as Merlot attests, Christian sorrow does not lead to despair. Despair, accordingly, is a loss of confidence, whereas repentance is faith regained.

This new outlook presents one with a test of choice. The glory of eternity is unveiled to the soul as a token during moments of spiritual purity. In contrast, the lure of the pleasures of this present life—which are defiled by the stench of death—stands upright before a person in disobedience and clamor. If one chooses the life hidden in God, his sins will be tossed into the sea of oblivion—thrown into eternal nonexistence—and will vanish. However, if one chooses to live in the present moment as a prisoner of pleasures, his soul will be heavy due to the chains of sin. He will fall to the lowest level of the temporal world, which rests on the chief of this world who has dominion over the darkness of this age. So, repentance is a choice based on our attitude.

Regarding the concept of repentance, Kallistos Ware writes in his book *The Inner Kingdom*:

> It (repentance) is not just regret for the past, But
> a fundamental transformation
> Of our outlook,
> And a new way of looking at ourselves,
> At others and at God...
> But not necessarily an emotional crisis,
> Repentance is not a paroxysm of remorse And
> self-pity, but conversion,
> The re-centering of our life
> Upon the Holy Trinity.
> It is not despondency but eager expectation...
> It is not to feel

That one has reached an impasse,

But to take the way out,

To repent is to look,

Not downward at my own shortcomings, But

upward at God's love;

Not backward with self-reproach,

But forward with trustfulness,

Repentance is to see,

Not what I have failed to be,

But, what by the grace of Christ

I can yet become.

It does not occur once,

It is a continuous attitude.

In reference to the divine approach of how the Lord addressed His people in the Old Testament, we find that the Israelites had not stopped offering sacrifices on the altar, until the coming of Jesus Christ, because sin had not stopped in their lives. When the Israelites stumbled in their paths, and tended toward a pattern of behavior and worshipping that belongs to the Gentiles, the Lord instructed them to offer sacrifices to atone for their sins. The Lord thus granted us repentance—which is the most pleasing sacrifice to Him—to us who became an abode of the Spirit, in order to restore the purity of our white gown of baptism, declaring to us that "the same Lord over all is rich to all who call upon Him" (Rom 10:12). When we seek mercy, God is always richer toward us than our greatest aspirations.

Regarding His rich grace that is bestowed endlessly, Saint John Chrysostom writes, in his *Commentary of the Gospel of Matthew* (118\4):

> Neither depleted nor mislaid is the grace; It is a perennial fountain.

If you request mercy, then He shall give it to you, as well as grace according to His riches. If you ask for salvation, He shall give it to you adorned with delight. If you take the least important place, He shall move you up to the king's table, and if you seek repentance, He shall grant it to you with holiness. God is always "able to do exceedingly abundantly above all that we ask or think" (Eph. 3:20); His gifts are always according to "His royal bounty" (1 Kings 10:13), not pursuant to what we ask or what servants are entitled to.

Transformation

●●●

The resounding and desert-filled cry of John the Baptist: "Repent, for the kingdom of heaven is at hand!" (Matt 3: 2), are the words that marked the beginning of a new covenant that became the door to the heavenly mysteries, yet not captivated by mere texts, charming characters, and human traditions. Repentance is the basis for creating the new Kingdom that Christ will announce in the hearts of those who have been drawn by the Spirit, and have become immersed in God and in the Kingdom.

The cry of John concerning repentance implied an invitation to conversion in preparation to accept the Messiah, who has no halo around His head, is not dressed in purple, does not carry a weapon, and is not supported by angelic forces to defeat the enemies. Rather, He came in the dusty clothes of a modest carpenter, and His sweat glistened from the hardships of the journey that He endured in the heat of the Jewish sun!

The repentance declared by John went beyond the penitence of sins. It is fundamentally a call for a mental shift to accept the unique Christ, who has not been ordained by priests, teachers of the law, or leaders of the people in an inadequate way.

Perhaps, in this distorted and confused era, we could draw from the Baptist's concept of repentance, in order to see it as an intellectual shift to accept the Messiah, unlike what we had envisaged according to our spiritual maturity. Hence, our repentance is connected with our bygone contentment in Christ, giving it a life emanating from the life of Christ itself; wherefore it brings satisfaction to the soul that asks for what is right amid the fogginess of falsehood, which is spreading dangerously in the minds of the current world.

Repentance, in this account, is a change from our past contentment and a shift in our current attitudes in search for Jesus. It is not a stage, but a permanent, continuous life pattern. It is a new law rather than a passing commandment. It is a human movement toward God, not an inactive absorption in grief and despair.

Neither Do I Condemn You

●●●

One morning, while Jesus was teaching in the temple and crowds were surrounding Him as usual, a group of Scribes and Pharisees went to Him amid the hustle and bustle of the people, and being followed by a gathering of the masses, they pushed before Him a young woman.

The woman seemed to be in her thirties, was of medium height with oriental features, and her face was hidden behind curls of hair scattered over her face on which tears were silently streaming down from her frightened and worried eyes, painting her face with a pale yellowness; disfiguring her features.

With severity the Scribes and Pharisees hurled accusations at the woman, and their speech was not void of words that included "Moses," "the Nomos," "fornication" and "stoning". Meanwhile, the face of that victim, that was thrown in the midst, was becoming even more pale.

The crowd started to gather and whisper together. Some of them pitied her, but their fear of the Scribes and Pharisees' attack made them bite their tongues and stay silent. Meanwhile, others were calling for enforcement of the punishment of the Nomos. The great majority of the people, however, were looking at Jesus who stooped down and began writing words on the ground with His finger. They were all waiting for the Teacher to say something.

That state of anticipation was felt not only the crowd, but also by the Scribes and Pharisees, who were stood arrogantly with eyes full of triumph and cunning.

If Jesus endorsed the stoning of that woman, He would join a group who supported the implementation of the Nomos; thereby losing the support of the people concerning His new vision of the meaning of the commandment. However, if He refused the punishment of the woman, He would be shown to be a disbeliever in the Nomos and against the Law. Thus, they would mobilize the masses against Him for being a disbeliever in the Nomos and ultimately He would become the prey!

These thoughts spurred the Scribes and Pharisees to bring that woman before Him.

Their resonant words; such as, "Why? Were they not the children of Judah, who made love to the wife of his son and regarded her as a prostitute?" And, "when he heard that his daughter-in-law had committed adultery, he said, 'Bring her out and have her burned to death'"

(Gen 38), were accurately quoted from the Pentateuch and were consistent with patristic tradition. Their intention was to give a speech confirming the necessity of punishment according to the Nomos, and thereby strike an accord with the Jewish community and with God by showing they shun the same sin He shuns.

Jesus raised Himself up, and with a voice full of grief and sorrow, said:

> He who is without sin among you, let him throw a stone at her first. (John 8:7)

Those unexpected words were like a stone that made the Scribes and Pharisees lose their balance. Their tongues were held and silence prevailed, in which Jesus stooped down and began to write once again on the ground. However, this time He stared at one of them before stooping down to write a word, and then looked at another one before writing another word, and so forth. The words that Jesus had written were titles for sins: seizure of widows, adultery, deceit, hypocrisy, and deviation from the rules... these were the most repeated words.

The elders began to leave one by one as if avoiding a scandal. Tension and anxiety were apparent on their faces that was obvious to all. A few minutes later, none of the Scribes and Pharisees remained at the scene. And no one remained except some people upon whom smiles were drawn on their kind faces. And their faces had not known such smiles of victory for a long time because they had only known grief.

Then they left, reassured that the woman was in compassionate hands. Jesus alone was left with the woman.

As fear began to fall away from the face of that woman, and timidity began to wash over the contours of her sad face, she tried to look up at Jesus to thank Him for saving her, and she glimpsed a purity that exposed her sin.

Jesus stood up and gave her a compassionate look that removed her timidity; a look she had never been given before, a look that kindled within her a longing for a life of purity, and restored the value of a life that had lost its way because it followed the manner of the beasts of the earth.

Jesus broke the silence and reserve, and said to her: Woman, where are those accusers of yours? Has no one condemned you?

She replied to Him, with head downcast: No one, Lord.

Jesus said to her:

> Neither do I condemn you;
>
> Go and sin no more. (John 8:10)

At that moment she felt overwhelming joy, as if the burdens of her past had suddenly evaporated, and her sins, which were always bothering her conscience, vanished away and were replaced by a longing for purity.

This is Jesus whom I have been long hearing about! Indeed, He is the Savior and Messiah! Those were her thoughts after Jesus went away.

About that story, the Lebanese author Adib Mousleh, writes in his book *Jesus in His Life* the following:

> The hands holding the sinful woman softened,
>
> And eyes were shamefully downcast,
>
> And the place became empty for only two,
>
> The sinful woman and the Savior
>
> (who have been described by St Augustine as
>
> "extreme misery and deep compassion").

In dealing with our sins, God does not adopt the strict attitude of the Scribes and Pharisees, as some people believe. He does not put the sinners' necks under the sword of punishment. He, however, chooses compassion to wash away sins and words of forgiveness. God is very affectionate. He longs for the return of a soul to Him. He knows that strict law does not attract souls, but divine kindness, that makes the sinner feel ashamed of his sins and desire that he offer himself completely as a sacrifice to the One who loves the soul unconditionally.

When a brother told Saint Macarius the Great:

Father, I sinned.

He replied:

Repent, my son,

Then you will see

The affection of our Lord Jesus Christ

And see His face fill with happiness.

This is the inherent Orthodox approach in encouraging one to repent. When the sinner feels the love of God, and sees Christ's face shining again in his life, he becomes determined to fight against his weaknesses so that he not suffer defeat. Thereafter, the chains of darkness are broken before the glory of love that awaits his return, and that glory softens his wounded heart, to restore life to it. Sophrony Sakharov attests:

> The grace of repentance
>
> Abducts the soul to God,
>
> As it is attracted to Him by His light.

Kallistos Ware adds:

> It is impossible to see our sins before Discerning
> the light of Christ

Repentance, then, means that our human being is attracted to the only source that carries a torch of hope amid the deep black darkness of the night. Here, the Savior comes with His ineffable light to bring the soul to the eternal light cycles, in which He will consolidate the beauty and joy of the new life away from darkness and sin. This is the experience that the penitent has during his daily journey, that he tries to escape the traps set for him and the arrows that are shot to make him fall.

Two French artists drew two pictures of the Prodigal Son. The first was by de Chavannes who in his picture focused on the son's miserable state, while the second artist, Rembrandt, focused on the father's attitude. In his book *Le Christ dans la thèologie de Saint Paul*, L. Cerfaux commented on the picture of Rembrandt, that the young man remains in the shadows giving his back to the viewer with his head on his father's lap. In the middle of the painting a light shines on the son's tattered clothes and worn shoes. The light seems to be emitted from the cheeks of his father and from his serene face and eyes that are full of affection that have been paled from many tears. The old man brings his coat to cover the misery of his lost son, and his trembling hands rest on the son's shoulders, in fear that he may leave again. Meanwhile, the eldest son stands aside with a cruel and frowning face, having contempt for the weakness of the father! Rembrandt genuinely discovered the central point in the parable, which is that of the compassionate father.

The fatherhood of God is the love that forms every divine movement toward us, although we are sinners. The beam of light emitted from His face while attending the moments of our sorrow over sin is the greatest motive for our rise, and the greatest attraction of our hearts toward the Kingdom.

Some may wonder why the Nomos, law and punishment exist!

Punishment is not for penitents; not for those who have hearts that just need the support and kindness of God to repent again. It is not for those who have the desire to follow God, while being attracted by the flesh to the world and not having the ability to avoid it, and it is not for those who seek God and read books until they are enlightened in their spiritual warfare so far as to taste victory.

On the other hand, punishment is reserved for the stubborn, as well as callous-hearted who do not feel the divine kindness. It is for those who have lost their common sense and who have mortified and buried their conscience! It is for those who are cruel and need the severity of God to turn them back to their senses and from their evil ways.

Kindness of God

•••

Have you ever meditated on the words of David the Prophet, who after the Lord had saved him from his enemies, he addressed God saying, "Your gentleness has made me great" (Ps. 18:35)? In the same way, Jesus had strengthened the heart of the sinful woman and He did not focus on her sin in order to magnify it for judgment, but He magnified her humility and contrite soul in order to grant her forgiveness.

In your life, God always looks for fruit, no matter how small, in order to praise, encourage, and accept it as being the first in a fruitful field that is full of diverse fruits of the Spirit. He searches for any sign to encourage and support us, so that we become like a large tree having birds lodging in its branches. And yet, why does God praise our two very small copper coins – our incomplete repentance, and our prayers that have not yet lived up to be the cries of the Spirit within us?

We find the answer is summed up in two words: submission and love. Submission and love are the two helms we raise high during our long journey. Complete submission to the Lord for Him to lead the helm of our life, so that we may achieve His will in accordance with human salvation. This is the only way to turn the balance, so that salvation wins, no matter what the obstacles are. The high winds that try to hit the ship of your life will turn when you resign your whole essence to the Trinity, to provide the impetus that accelerates your path so as to land on the shore of life. The wind will carry you as if you are on the wings of angels who are sent by God to give you help and protection. You will see that the wind, with all its unruliness and rigor, will not be able to deprive you of the salvation prepared for you. It will not become an obstacle on the path because the Lord's will is hidden there. The winds of trials will lead you to shores that are not foreseen in your journey. Yet, on those shores you will see that you have a duty to fulfill, and this shift in the path is the journey itself that the Lord has arranged to add weight to the glory prepared for you in eternity.

The trap, which Satan will set for you, will turn into a fortified wall. The waters that flooded Pharaoh and his soldiers were the waters that became a wall to the children of Israel during the most historic and famous Red Sea crossing. But you must first deliver the helm of your soul to the Lord in order to fight and cross the seas of trials. Then He will send His sword (His word) to destroy your enemies. No one will stand before you, as long as you believe that God can deliver you; and you, through Christ, can do everything—everything in the context of repentance.

> And the waters returned and covered the chariots
> and the horsemen and all the army of Pharaoh
> that came into the sea after them;
> Not so much as one of them remained.
> But the children of Israel
> Walked upon dry land in the midst of the sea;
> And the waters were a wall unto them on their
> right hand, and on their left (Ex 14: 28-29).

The love of God comes to emphasize the primary principle (submission). Love covers all sins, kindles the spirit, and leads us to God along the shortest routes.

David declared his love for the mighty God at the beginning of the Psalm, which he wrote to thank and praise the Lord who saved him from the hands of Saul who was chasing him: "I love you, O Lord, my strength" (Ps 18: 1). It expresses the longing of a heart that wants to be embodied in lyrics. It is a declaration of love that was born again from the womb of victory. And that victory is not achieved by human power, but it is by the divine strength intertwined in our lives, touching the human in his weakness and confusion, so that it supports him to rise, fight and win.

Hence, the love toward the Lord, which fills the heart, must be accompanied by a declaration of the soul's trust in His guidance in life, and then the soul will behold the eyes of God that magnifies the few—"for nothing restrains the Lord from saving by many or by few" (1 Sam 14: 6).

The love that grows from the fertile land of submission alone can make up for the lack of quantity! A short prayer, filled with yearning and the need for God, that is generated from the midst of a fierce struggle with Satan who is trying in various ways to mislead us regarding the chamber of prayer, is better than a long, apathetic prayer that comes out of the illusion of false peace, devolving into self-righteous growth inside the soul, distancing it from God once it imagines that it is praying in His presence!

When love becomes our law while dealing with God, and submission is our attitude to everything that confronts us in life, then kindness becomes God's telescope that enlarges our little works, develops and makes them fruitful virtues. That is the real victory, that is conditional on our ability to love and submit. The victory that we seek during our journey toward Christ, comes when He is the master of the soul and its leader. Thus, Saint Macarius says:

> When the Lord takes the helm of the soul
> By his hands,
> He always gains victory,
> Since He leads the soul skillfully,
> To an inspiring heavenly mind forever.

If we have that heavenly mind, which creates the Spirit within us, when Christ receives the helm of the self, we begin to be liberated from sin and recognize the face of Jesus, and here begins the repentance.

A State of Sin

●●●

The failure that overtakes us in our daily life—that we define as "sin"—is not the final part of our story. Everyone among us sins: "No one is without sin even if his life is only a day on earth," as recited (by the priest) in the liturgy. Yet the real danger is to remain in a state of sin—to make failure a daily, frequent attitude as if it is a creed we embrace—for in so doing it has the serious consequence of making us feel no compunction, or sorrow in our hearts when sin is committed. Such a state is a conscious halt of the daily struggle against lust, weakness and defeat. It is a cessation of repentance, resulting in us relishing the lust, and allying ourselves to it in order not to enter the war against it. That war may be associated with some losses of what we love and are bound by, and this is the misgiving that makes many people flee from the battlefield. It is the fear of losing what they might have been connected with in their life, and therefore what may have been considered as a necessity. This leads the sinner to stop living as he undergoes spiritual death in the same way as clinical death, which some patients experience, and they come closer to death than life. Spiritual death is a state of dryness in the inner essence, where the springs of pure blood that supply the new human's heart—which is born of water and the Spirit as well as the spiritual presence— become dry as a result of losing the connection with the source of life: Jesus the Savior.

In his message to Theodore, Saint John Chrysostom emphasizes that the loss caused by falling is less harmful than the state of falling:

> The fall of man is not a cause for sadness
>
> But rather, lingering long in the fall.

He then adds:

> To make a mistake is a human weakness,
>
> But to continue in sin,
>
> It is no longer a human matter, but diabolical.

Also, Saint Mark the Hermit, in his article about the real cause of judgment, writes:

> We are not condemned to our many trespasses,
>
> But because of our refusal to repent.

Undoubtedly the man who commits sin, and the sin in his life turns from a passing situation into a permanent state, turns into a wandering spirit with no hope or insight, and no higher goal to attract him away from the pleasures in which he is willingly indulging in. Here comes the Devil to feast on the walls of this pale heart that is suffering from the heaviness of sin. Then, the person becomes an abode of darkness, which largely increases until it reaches its full spiritual blindness; and Saint Paul describes this state as follows: "Whose minds the god of this age has blinded, who do not believe, lest the light of the gospel of the glory of Christ, who is the image of God, should shine on them " (2 Cor 4: 4).

When the light of hope in a heart fades away, the heart turns to stone and becomes an altar on which the demons offer various kinds of unclean sacrifices; and the sinner finds himself in the grave of lust, chained and a prisoner of sin and trespass, deprived of the right to hope, for darkness has robbed him of his most basic rights, namely thinking and self-determination.

And Satan, by recognizing the danger that hope has on his kingdom spreading everywhere, did not give attention to the sin as much as to the psychology of the sinner. After a human falls into sin, Satan starts to play his most devious role, which is to shut the door of hope to the sinner. By his black shrewdness, Satan begins to convince the soul that the light of life cannot dwell again in a body inhabited by sins, and the holy God will not listen again to the prayers of a sinner that has trodden on the blood of promise, and disdained grace, and denied the Son of God because of lust. Then when Satan succeeds in persuading the soul with the impossibility of return, or at least with its difficulty, he rejoices in making a soul fall into the most serious sin that the Lord had previously warned us of: the sin of blasphemy against the Holy Spirit; "Therefore I say to you, every sin and blasphemy will be forgiven men, but the blasphemy against the Spirit will not be forgiven men" (Mt 12:31).

Essentially, blasphemy against the Holy Spirit is due to a lack of faith in His ability to change the human condition from a person whose heaviness of darkness leads him to the abyss that attracts him by the power of sin, to a person who is capable of being free, dusting himself off of his sins and choosing his path toward the kingdom of penitents. When a person loses his confidence in the Holy Spirit, accordingly, he loses faith in the only Helper that can lift him out of the pit, and he remains lonely, surrounded only by the birds of despair who carry him to the port of death. Meanwhile, Satan, who was able to deceive the soul and obscure not only the light of hope but also the strength of hope, is gloating. Regarding blasphemy against the Holy Spirit,

St Augustine writes (in *NPNF*; vol. V, sermon 21):

Impenitent hearts

Utter words against the Holy Spirit,

Against this free grace,

And against the divine grace.

Lack of repentance is a blasphemy

Against the Holy Spirit

That will not be forgiven neither in this world

Nor in the coming.

Consequently, the Devil's most serious work is the demolition of the golden bridge (which is the work of the Holy Spirit) that connects our hearts, which are tiring in worldly conflict, with the heart of God that is filled with succor. This was experienced by Judah when his sin was magnified and he belittled the ability of the Holy Spirit to wash away that sin. Therefore, the rope of despair was Satan's advice to him, which he accepted and hence died in his sin. Meanwhile, God's heart ached over a man that did not trust in the Spirit, or depend on His grace, or hold on to hope. As a consequence, he was swept away toward the fate of sinners and blasphemers of the Spirit of God!

Galeno and F. Doner wrote in their book *Rebellious Youth* that:

> Despair is an empty, meaningless word,
>
> To the one who has a youthful heart,
>
> And an immortal soul,
>
> And a god who loves him.

So how can you feel despair when you have God, whose essence is love? His words are spirit and life, and His action is always focused on humankind. How can you allow such a feeling to sneak into your heart in moments of sin and weakness when you know by heart the words of Micah the Prophet that bring hope and build the fallen soul: "Do not rejoice over me, my enemy; when I fall, I will arise; when I sit in darkness, the Lord will be a light to me" (Micah 7: 8)? How do you accept defeat to darkness when you know that the light is close to you? It is closer to you than your own breath! How do you throw out your weapon in battle when you realize that there is a crowd of blazing servants (who are the heavenly powers) who will defend you once you raise your eyes toward heaven and let out your heart's cries, which are able to shake the heart of the Heavenly Father who is awaiting your call in order to lead the war instead of you. He is waiting to be your shield of salvation, rock of shelter, and stronghold of protection?

Why do you despair when you have read about the sinful woman who threw herself at the feet of Jesus, and shed tears on them, and Jesus forgave her long history of sin?

Saint John Chrysostom attests to the effectiveness of tears that are shed from the eyes of hope, saying:

> Holy tears are the seeds of lasting joy
> Thus the sinful woman became more
> Honorable than the Virgins,
> Who did not hold onto this fire...
> When she was filled with the
> Warmth of repentance
> She became overjoyed
> In her love for Christ
> She left her hair loose and washed
> His pure feet with her tears
> And wiped them with the locks of her hair,
> These are external fruits
> But what occurred in her heart,
> Was more passionate than that,
> Things only beheld by God.

If you hear about the passion of the Spirit that was aflame in the hearts of the saints, and you long for and desire to experience that purified fire, but your reality is wrapped in a cool shroud and marred by weakness and defeatism; do not despair. The tears of repentance are able to restore life to your heart, which had been inhabited by coolness for a long time, so that you may feel the beauty of the passion of the Spirit that is inflamed by grace, when grace tests the credibility of your tears.

Saint John of Sinai, in his book *The Ladder of Divine Ascent* (the fifth step), writes:

> Nothing equals or excels God's mercies. Therefore, he who despairs is committing suicide.

From now on, you should delete the word "despair" from the dictionary of your life. As long as you breathe, there is hope; there is resurrection, and there is revival. God is always waiting for your return, whatever your state is.

Saint Gregory of Nazianzus, in his sermon *About Epiphany*, urges:

> I wish you would fall into the arms of repentance rather than the arms of despair.

Between Two Falls

•••

In the beginning of the spiritual journey, our struggle is boiled down to two key actions:

- The attempt to reduce the time between two acts of repentance, thus prolonging the time between two acts of fall; and

- The attempt to give more attention to the little sins that seem to be a minor fall and can be minimized at any time.

Those who start their spiritual life are beset by dangers, as they think that when they fall into sin repeatedly, they must give up because all is futile and that the spiritual life is further to reach than when they embraced the world!

So, those who take the first step toward a life with God, wearing the garment of repentance, must be diligent to hasten their penitence whenever they fall, and not to give heed to the murmurings of the Devil who wants to make them indulge in sin. He intends to give the feeling that the action of standing before God is for those who are behaviorally and morally committed, and who have never fallen before! This is because Satan is afraid that the sinner's period of being in a state of repentance becomes longer than the periods of his being in the state of sin. Nonetheless, if the sinner recognizes that the most powerful way to respond to sin is to repent as soon as possible, then the Devil finds that the time of repentance in the life of that person represents the bulk of his life in spite of falling frequently. And the penitent, consequently, reaps countless crowns!

Therefore, do not be slow to rise for prayer and to admit sins and weakness, even if the smell of sin has not been removed from your clothes yet!

In the *Paradise of the Fathers*, we read a wonderful story about the insistence of hope in spite of falling:

> [A story] about a brother who was dwelling in the monastery. He fell repeatedly due to the intensity of warfare. He kept forcing himself to be patient in order not to abandon the monastic skema. He was diligent in his monastic life and said his prayers carefully. In his prayer he would say: 'O Lord, You see the severity of my state and my deep sorrow. Rescue me, O Lord, whether I am

willing or unwilling, because I am like clay and I yearn for and love sin. But You are the Great God, remove impurity from me, because if You only have mercy on saints, this will not be strange. And if You only save the pure ones, then what will be the benefit, for they are already worthy. However, reveal the wonder of Your mercy in me, the unworthy, O my Lord, because I have submitted myself to You.' This is the prayer he said every day, whether he committed a fault or not. One day, as he prayed fervently, Satan became weary of the boldness of his great hope, and as he chanted his Psalms, a face appeared to him, saying: 'Do you not feel ashamed of standing before God and mentioning His name with your impure mouth?' The brother responded: Do you not strike with a sledgehammer and I do likewise? You cause me to fall into sin, and I ask the merciful God to take pity on me. I struggle against you, until l am overtaken by death. I will cling onto hope from my God and will not cease from being prepared for your attacks, and thus you will witness who wins: you or God's mercy.

When the Devil heard his words, he said: 'From now on, I will not fight you, lest I give you crowns because of your hope in your God.' From that day, the Devil kept away from him.

On the other hand, we find that one of the dangers that interrupts our repentance is when we save our attention and efforts for 'big' sins. Accordingly, we suffer delay spiritually because we are unaware that when 'little' sins accumulate they may cause more harm on our spiritual journey.

Hence, the English writer, C. S. Lewis, in his book *The Screwtape Letters* writes letters through uses the spokesman Screwtape (who is a senior demon), to write letters of advice to his nephew Wormwood (who is a Junior Tempter) on how to secure the damnation of humankind, saying:

> The only thing that matters
> Is the extent to which you separate
> The man from the Enemy (i.e. God)
> It does not matter how small the sins are,
> Provided that their cumulative effect
> Is to edge the man away from the Light
> And out into the Nothing...

Indeed the safest road to Hell is

The gradual one—the gentle slope,

Soft underfoot, without sudden turnings,

Without milestones, without signposts.

(Book 12)

So, one of the Devil's titles is "Ropemaker", because he makes the human separate himself, bit by bit, from his goal without feeling it. In doing so, the Devil depends on two factors; namely:

- The length of time.
- Shifting the path of repentance to focus on the big sins, which are often symptoms of an internal disease in the heart, which have arisen from the accumulation of little sins.

The Holy Bible has warned us: "Catch us the foxes, the little foxes that spoil the vines, for our vines have tender grapes" (Songs 2:15). The danger lies in the results that eventuate from our lack of attention to such sins. Repentance is the awareness of sin as a wall that separates humankind from God. Whether this wall is high or not, it remains a wall that needs to be demolished by the pickaxe of repentance.

Light of Hope

•••

The role of the Holy Spirit in repentance is to send signals to the person from whom Satan tries to hide the truth of hope. Those signals may be in multiple forms and patterns, but you will always find yourself saying these words within your heart:

You are beloved from the outset.

You are as precious as the blood

That was shed for you.

You are the child of light.

You are the fruit of the resurrection.

You were born for eternity.

You are the beautiful image of God on earth.

Rise and hold on to hope in the Lord,

Bow down before the Spirit of Truth,

Accept His advice for repentance,

Be humble in the hands of the Lord,

So His hands carry you, and you hold

His right hand that is glorified by power.

So the self finds the rays of hope returning again after the false allegations by which Satan was hiding the truth of hope. Truth is capable of breaking the chains of sin just as the sun melts particles of snow on foliage at sunrise.

The Holy Spirit begins to revive a person's spiritual memory through bringing to mind what has been recorded in Christian history regarding sinners who have been liberated from the graves of lust and transferred to spiritual pastures near the Sun of eternal life.

Who has knocked on the doors of our compassionate God's mercies and He left them to suffer in fear and loneliness?

Who has implored and not found hosts of angels of light sent by the Lord to defend that single soul whom no one has cared for?

Who has longed and thirsted in their heart for God, and God has not reciprocated with even greater longing?

Who, having a bloody wound that was prolonged in the battle of life, did not lift his eyes toward Heaven, beseeching the Greatest Physician, and did not find the Son of righteousness bringing healing on its wings (Mal 4:2)?

Who cried out to heaven, "Lord, to whom shall we go? You have the words of eternal life" (John 6:68), and not find that the Lord's home is ready, the Lord's banquet prepared, and life-giving words coming to settle in his heart?

Who has returned from the pigs' village after losing his inheritance, and did not find the Father longingly coming out to meet him in the middle of the road, holding his hands, seating him down at the table of forgiveness, and give him back the ring of sonship?

Who has touched the edge of the Lord's garments and not gained power to be rid of impurities?

Who has knelt down in front of the Lord, being condemned by the world and wounded by all, and not find the Lord defending him and reproaching those condemned him? Above all, the Lord leaves him forgiven, with peace, power, and support.

Who has thought of the enormity of sin and forgotten that there is a divine sea into which sins and misdeeds are cast into and forgotten, never to return again because the Lord is pleased with casting them out?

Who has stumbled in his spiritual blindness and not found the Lord's hands creating for him new insight so that he may discern by faith what he had not seen by day?

Who has loved the Lord more than the Lord loves them?

The Church has documented examples of sinners who were drowning in sins, but because of their hope and trust in the Lord, and their complete submission to the guidance of the Holy Spirit, they became living witnesses that sin is not a hindrance as long as it is followed by repentance. In fact, the Spirit uses sins to form within us a genuine repentance and firmly-established conviction.

Thus, Saint John of Sinai said:

> You have blessed those who fell and lamented
> More than those who did not fall
> Nor lament.

We find in the biographies of Saint Moses the Black, Saint Augustine, Saint Mary of Egypt, and Saint Thais of the Desert, examples of spirited repentance and how it has the power to make one cross over the mountains of sin, no matter how high are they, and extract the roots of evil, no matter how deeply they have penetrated into the heart of a person. Here, our testimony is not about special human capabilities, nor aptitudes that distinguish those people from us. Rather, it concerns the infinite ability of the Holy Spirit to transfer the sheep who are on the left, to lambs who sit at the right hand of the Father. This testimony also exhibits the divine door that is never closed in the face of supplicants. It attests to a heart that, when the soul repents and returns, has room for all humankind and forgets the ugliness of the past and the hardship of bygone days. In addition, it attests to the sincerity of Christ's call, that: "the one who comes to Me I will by no means cast out." (John 6:37). Also, it witnesses to a late hour—maybe the eleventh—in which many are rescued from the fire of judgment and brought to the rivers of the Spirit, where they experience divine love.

The Battle is the Lord's

●●●

The Devil cannot seize the land that has been submerged by the water of baptism and consecrated by Chrism, as long as it is guarded by repentance. He may win in a battle, cast some seeds of tares, or send his winds to make fruit fall, but he cannot own that land, as long as on this land sacrifices are being offered day and night: the sacrifices of supplication and invocation to receive help from heaven. As long as our hearts do not stop crying out, we must not be afraid of anything, because grace and help will come. If darkness falls on us during our journey, the Lord is the light who will illuminates our path. One cannot be afraid of the uncertainty of darkness when the Lord's light illuminates his way, and leads his steps so that he may not fall.

Accordingly, the main measure in repentance is one's capability to stick to the weapon of prayer, in spite of the wounds weakening our spiritual body. As long as one hopes for heavenly support, enemies will be afraid because falling and crying out will be regarded as struggle, and thus a crown of glory will be granted as long as one does not succumb to the pressure of sin, which endeavors to prevent prayers from rising toward heaven.

When the soul falls into sin and then repents, it raises many questions: Will my repentance continue after falling repeatedly? Can I resist in the battlefield after breaking all the vows and promises that accompany my repentance every time? Will I be able to stand against the soldiers of evil who prevent my penitence? Can I avoid the flaming arrows of Satan that are being shot from all directions?

However, the questions should be, in fact: Can the Lord triumph within me over the soldiers of the realm of darkness? Can He turn the furnace of fire around me into cool dew?

In our repentance, the first thing that we must learn is that the battle is the Lord's, and the Lord is able to destroy our enemies by a word of His mouth. Therefore, we must not be engrossed in wars of tomorrow and our destiny—will we fall or resist? Our role in each moment is to praise the work of the Lord related to His support for us. Tomorrow is the Lord's. Likewise, Moses and the children of Israel praised the Lord for the salvation that they witnessed, giving no attention to tomorrow, the difficulty of the journey, the danger of the path, or the hardship of desert. Today is the day of praise for being rescued from the evil of Pharaoh. But as for tomorrow, it is the Lord's.

The Church grasped this praise very early and made it the first fruit of praises in the Church (the First Ode in the Midnight Praise according to the Coptic Rite), to declare it as a way that should be lived and followed consistently. The praise of victory is capable of destroying the evil surrounding us, and this praise also ignites the spirit with hope and brings stability into the life of the congregation so that they are not afraid of the dangers of tomorrow. Today's praise is tomorrow's shield against enemies. It is a sword of victory that girds the soul every night, as long as it continues to praise and chant. It is the royal garment of praise that Isaiah spoke about: instead of the spirit of heaviness, praise is able to return you back once more to fight in the front-line of battle and win.

> To console those who mourn in Zion, to give them beauty for ashes, The oil of joy for mourning, the garment of praise for the spirit of heaviness; that they may be called trees of righteousness, the planting of the Lord, that He may be glorified. (Is 61:3)

Open your Holy Bible to Genesis 15:1-18 and pray this praise. I invite you now to listen with your heart to these words. Try to touch and taste the victory and delight when the people were rescued from Pharaoh and his soldiers. Try to make it your own praise when you feel afraid of falling. Simply praise with these words until you see the victory of the Lord in your life, and do not let them tire in your mouth.

Finally, I will leave you with the words of Habakkuk the Prophet, which are full of hope, in spite of the difficult challenges faced in the present that do not seem to have even a glimmer of light!

> Though the fig tree may not blossom,
> Nor fruit be on the vines;
> Though the labor of the olive may fail,
> And the fields produce no food,
> Though the flock may be cut off from the fold,
> And there be no herd in the stalls
> Yet I will rejoice in the Lord,
> I will joy in the God of my salvation.
> The Lord God is my strength;
> He will make my feet like deer's feet,
> And He will make me walk on my high hills.
> (Hab 3:17-19)

Conclusion

●●●

A wise man once said:

    Hope is a powerful principle for action,

    To achieve complete humanity.

Now we need a new strategy for repentance by which we may confront our enemies who throw nets of despair on the land of the living, and hunt daily those whom Christ died for. We need a strategy of complete confidence and assurance in God; a strategy of permanent cries that penetrate through the clouds of despair and darkness of sin; cries of prayers at all times and everywhere, without paying attention to our desperate state. Crying is our means to change our state through the power of grace. Indeed, we need a strategy of hope that is similar to steady rocks. Hope is the soul's anchor when it is swept by waves and is on the verge of doom and drowning. Hope that yearns for salvation is the weapon by which we win the battle. It is the weapon that the forces of darkness cannot withstand.

Through the enlightenment of his spiritual awakening, Saint Paul the Apostle stressed the importance of this hope in the struggle between light and darkness, saying: "For we were saved in this hope" (Rom. 8:24). Repentance without hope is a journey without light that ends at the cliff of despair. It is a journey led by the Devil, in accordance with his plan for the destruction of humankind!

Regarding the torch of hope, Charles Peguy wrote:

There is a torch that nothing can extinguish,

Neither can a person put it out,

Because this torch is unchanging,

And stronger than death.

"For You will light my lamp; the Lord my God will enlighten my darkness" (Psalm 18:28). No matter how intense and how long the darkness persists, the light of the Lord will continue to be stronger than the darkness of sin. When He comes, He will announce to the soul: "I am the light of the world. He who follows Me shall not walk in darkness, but have the light of life" (John 8:12). He will give you the light of life.

Moreover, when He comes, He will carry you to the right life: "He makes my feet like the feet of a deer" (Psalm 18:33). You will overcome lust, and during your journey to the spring of light, your eyes will be opened to the power of the Savior: "Uphold my steps in Your paths, that my footsteps may not slip"(Psalm 17:5); "You will show me the path of life; in Your presence is fullness of joy; at Your right hand are pleasures forevermore" (Psalm 16:11).

"We will rejoice in your salvation and in the name of our God we will set up our banners!" (Ps 20:5). This banner is a testimony to the whole world, and is written by the blood of love that flows from the Cross.

All who have this hope in Him,
purify themselves (1 John 3: 3).

Nuggets about Repentance

●●●

• Repentance is a retrieval of bursts of light that our hearts lost when we went down to a world of misery and grief after our fall. It washes away the impurities of darkness that were knitted by our desires and instincts and attached themselves to our essence; the essence that was formed in the divine image. These bursts of light were seized by Satan who rendered them a dense forest to stop the light of life from passing through our awareness and insight.

• Repentance is a return to the Lord who awaits His beloved humankind that He formed as a beautiful, pure icon, dressed in the glory of righteousness, before it had been distorted by the arrows of sin that turned it to a major offence walking on two legs.

• Christ's total call and daily cry was "repent," because repentance is a new meeting that gathers together humankind requesting water from dry wells, and to sit with Him at the spring of life.

• The Kingdom cannot be stepped into except by the person who is wrapped in the gown of repentance to cover the nakedness of his sin. In the same way that light will not meet with darkness under the dome of life, which is in Christ.

• Repentance is the water that washes the eyes that are unable to distinguish between light and darkness. It is a new pool of Siloam recommended by Christ to those who have lost the insight and ability to distinguish between the way of life and the way of death.

• Repentance is to irrevocably return one's feelings about the value of time that goes by, and testifies to whoever accepted sin and dwelled in it for long nights. It is a shock to the human consciousness that forgets the flow of time and believes that it controls everything, as if time could come back again, giving the opportunity for one to tear apart the agreement of slavery that was forged between the soul and Satan in unholy moments of pleasure. How impossible is it for time to come back, and for Satan to return the agreement of slavery if there is a divine hand to grab the right to life from his claws? This divine hand will only move when it witnesses the truth of our return, the groanings of our hearts, and our longing for and hope to see the light again. He will save the remaining time of life we have to make it an asset of righteousness that angels lift up on the greatest day when one crosses over from this present life to his origin in God.

• Repentance is the restoration of joy in hearts; hearts that only knew laughter that comes out of a mouth controlled by sin, as it brings forth bitterness in cold, pale laughter that joy did not pass by nor hope touch.

• Repentance is a cry to the Spirit of God to once again be the Heavenly King to a soul that had accepted the kingdom of Satan for a long time and lived in the paths of pleasure and frivolity, and under the scepter of wickedness.

• Repentance is a human declaration of the temporal nature of the physical world that captures our minds, besieges our understandings, and refuses to grant us the self-determination to choose another higher and eternal world.

• Repentance is just a human cry to escape from the present world's prison in spite of its gilded bars and walls.

• Repentance means seeing Jesus once again after a long absence.

• Repentance is not related to the bygone moment as much as the present moment.

• Repentance is the practical certainty of the incarnation.

• While the world talks about societal peace, it remains far from reality because it can only be attained by the gathering together of penitent hearts.

• Only repentance can untie the ropes of darkness that are around the human body, and seize the power of the Resurrection from the Savior's mouth who says "Come out." Then the soul may shake off the lethargy of darkness to see an affectionate God who is near, and who is only pleased with the rescue and salvation of His beloved ones.

• Repentance is being strengthened by Christ in the face of the present world.

• Repentance is a testimony to the authenticity of the Bible's call, and its suitability for the modern era and contemporary mind.

• Only the sacrifice of repentance is able to gladden the heavenly gathering that is watching the salvation of humankind.

• The problem lies in our human stubbornness that does not give Christ the opportunity to fight for us in the battle of life. It is the stubbornness intoxicated by life that has become confused and can no longer distinguish light from darkness. This is because darkness adorned itself with semi-garments of light and played with the senses, tying them by secret ropes, which then increase to become traps; at the center of which is the abyss, and the captor is the prince of the air.

• Repentance is the fruit of a partnership between grace and a human. Without that partnership, it is impossible to find peace that brings about repentance.

• Christian love is the essence of the Biblical call. However, love remains impractical if it does not pass across the penitent's heart toward God and people.

• Repentance is a mustard seed given by Christ to the land of humanity so that it can restore the glory of sonship lost by sin.

• The Eucharistic repentance that we practice during the liturgy is the shortest way to reach peace of the heart.

• Repentance without eschatological aspirations is a momentary declamatory attitude.

• The greatest testimony that we can present to the world about the Lord is our repentance.

• Superficial repentance is one of the greatest obstacles that make our repentance a circular path with no port.

• If incarnation has opened the sealed door between earth and heaven, repentance revives the action of incarnation in hearts that have been closed by sin before the call of the Spirit.

• Repentance could not be accepted without the incarnation of the Son. And without human penitence, there is no active incarnation.

• The whole world is waiting for our repentance to evaluate the message of salvation that Christ carried by His incarnation!

• Saying the Jesus prayer is an effective way to plant seeds of repentance in the heart of the man who is presently immersed in the world's bustling seas that do not subside.

• True repentance is dynamic in the heart, even if it is hidden behind a dormant body.

• The contemporary mind cannot evaluate life by a measure of productivity, as if to see the act of repentance and its impact on the human entity. Only spiritual insight is able to feel the need of repentance within a person as a life-flowing spring that does not stop and is not conditional on materialistic productivity.

• Repentance is a moment of genuine prayer.

• The Devil strives hard to keep us away from the places that urge us to repent and lead us to repentance. The chamber of prayer, the church and monastery are places that kindle feelings of repentance, therefore, Satan wants to pluck us from them, so that he can be alone with us in the outer wilderness of darkness where his victory is guaranteed when our weapons of repentance are absent.

• Repentance means wearing the rope of discipleship once again, and sitting at the feet of the greatest teacher, Jesus.

• Effectiveness of repentance lies in what we should be, not in what we should practice.

• O Lord, Jesus Christ, Son of the Living God, have mercy on me, a sinner! These were the constant cries of repentance that came out of Egyptian monastic caves in the 4th century. Thus, the wilderness was on fire through the work of the Spirit.

• The Son tells us about the Father, and no one sees the Father without the Son, and the Spirit attests to the Son in our hearts, who only dwells within penitent hearts. Hence, without repentance we cannot see the Trinity, and understand theology.

• Repentance is the human declaration that, "We want to see Jesus."

• Repentance is an intense thirst for the water of life.

• Sin's deadly effect on humankind is only realized by the penitents.

• Repentance is when the human crosses the boundaries of his isolation to the collective salvation and eternal reunion.

• Human repentance is the penitence of the sinful person.

• Orthodox repentance is not of a legal nature to satisfy God; rather, it has a remedial nature that seeks one's recovery so as to see God.

• Repentance is the best way a human can thank the Divine One for salvation.

• Repentance is the human way to attract the divine spirit in an attempt to develop a deeper awareness and to be connected with eternity.

• Repentance is a life-long daily march.

• Patristic teachings speak of Christ as a physician for humankind, and so accordingly, the medication prescribed for daily life, is repentance.

• Repentance is a most vital weapon that Satan resists with vigor, because in a moment of union between humankind and the Trinity, it strips Satan of life gained.

• Repentance is a change of mind followed by a change in the attitudes and contentment in our life.

• Repentance reinstates Jesus to His original position as the center of life and existence.

• Repentance brings back the person once again to Church, and renews his membership into the body of Christ (the Church) that sees the Kingdom.

• Repentance is based on faith that the sun that sets today will inevitably rise again.

Made in the USA
Middletown, DE
18 March 2025

72914869R00060